WE HEART HARRY

WE HEART HARRY

WE HEART HARRY

WE HEART HARRY

50 REASONS YOUR DREAM BOYFRIEND

HARRY STYLES IS PERFECTION

HARRY

Smith Street Books

WE HEART

50 REASONS YOUR DREAM BOYFRIEND

HARRY STYLES IS PERFECTION

HARRY

Harry was only 16 when he auditioned for *The X Factor*, singing Stevie Wonder's *"ISN'T SHE LOVELY"* a capella.

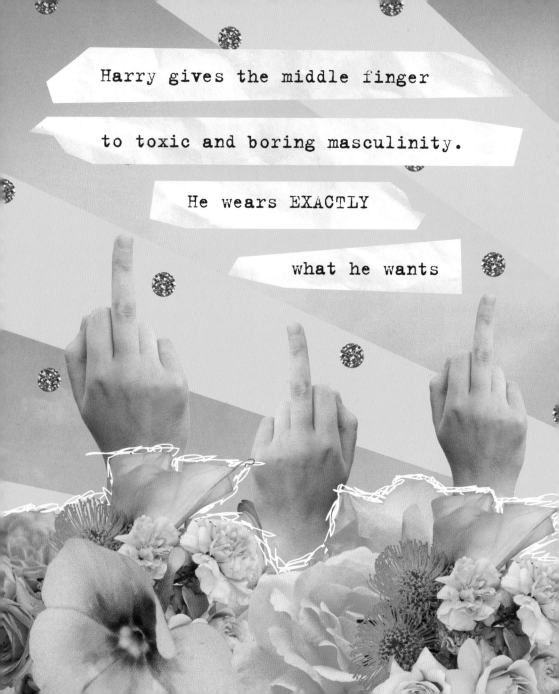

Harry gives the middle finger

to toxic and boring masculinity.

He wears EXACTLY

what he wants

AND LOOKS...

FABULOUSSS.

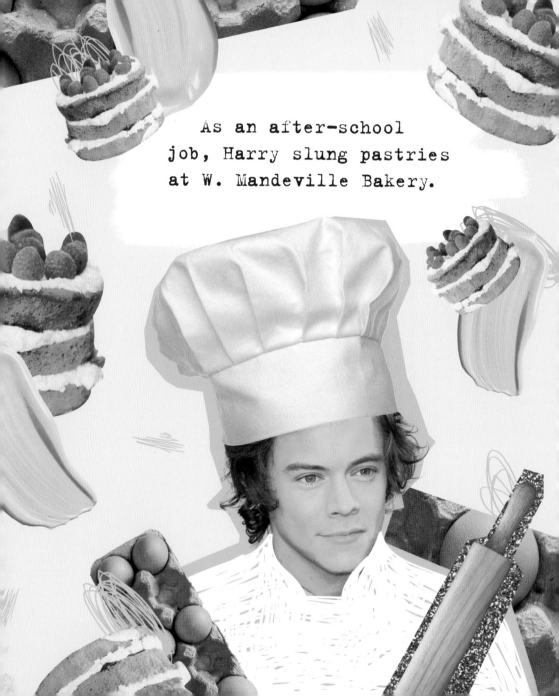

As an after-school job, Harry slung pastries at W. Mandeville Bakery.

His former boss said that "He was the most polite member of staff we've ever had."

IS ANYONE EVEN SURPRISED?

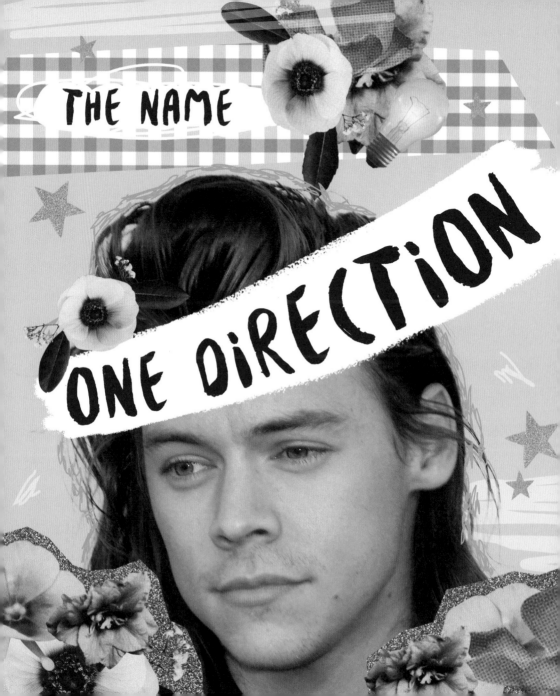

THE NAME

ONE DiRECTiON

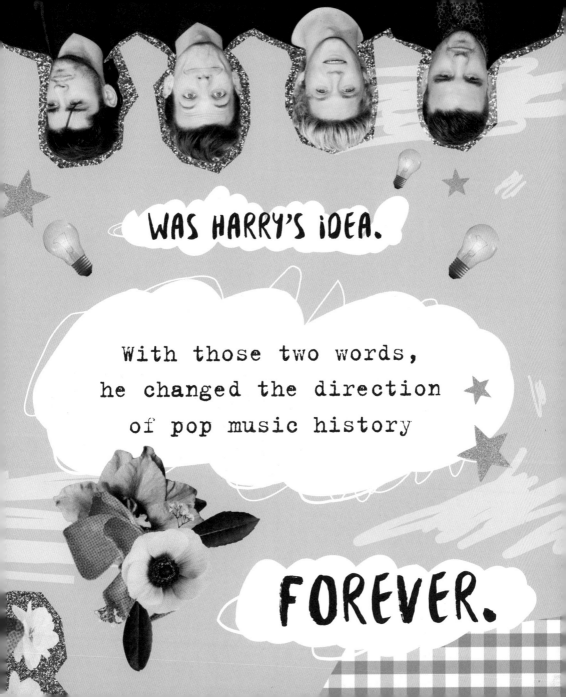

WAS HARRY'S iDEA.

With those two words,
he changed the direction
of pop music history

FOREVER.

Harry is unabashedly schmaltzy.

He loves romcoms and his favorite films are tear-jerkers — The Notebook, Love Actually, and Titanic.

PASS THE TISSUES,

PLEASE.

He's an

AQUARIUS.

As a fellow air sign,
that makes us a perfect

COSMIC MATCH.

(JUST SAYiN...)

One Direction never won
The X Factor.

Instead,

they came third

and proceeded to casually take over

THE WORLD,

becoming one of the best-selling

boy bands

OF ALL TIME.

Growing up, Harry had a pet hamster.

In a sign of the creativity that would make him into a **MEGASTAR,**

HARRY NAMED IT... **HAMSTER.**

His fisrt celebrity crush was

JENNIFER ANISTON.

I would ship
that couple.

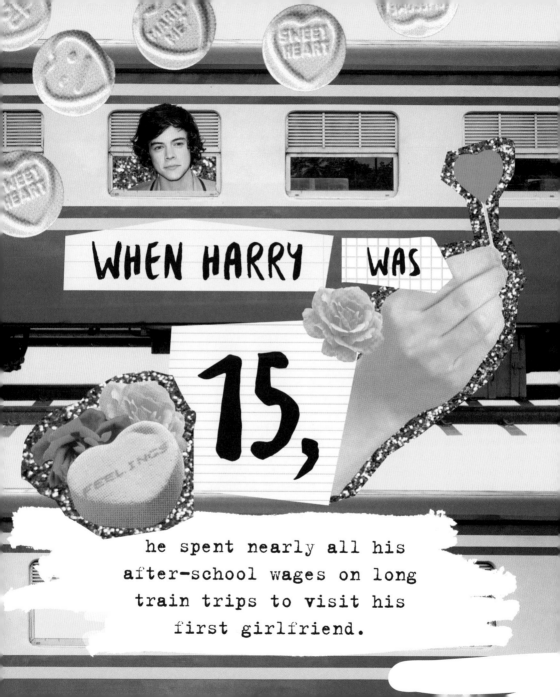

WHEN HARRY WAS

15,

he spent nearly all his
after-school wages on long
train trips to visit his
first girlfriend.

Harry stands up for his legions of superfans:

"How can you say young girls don't get it?

They're our future.

Our future doctors,

lawyers,

mothers,

presidents.

They kind of keep the world going."

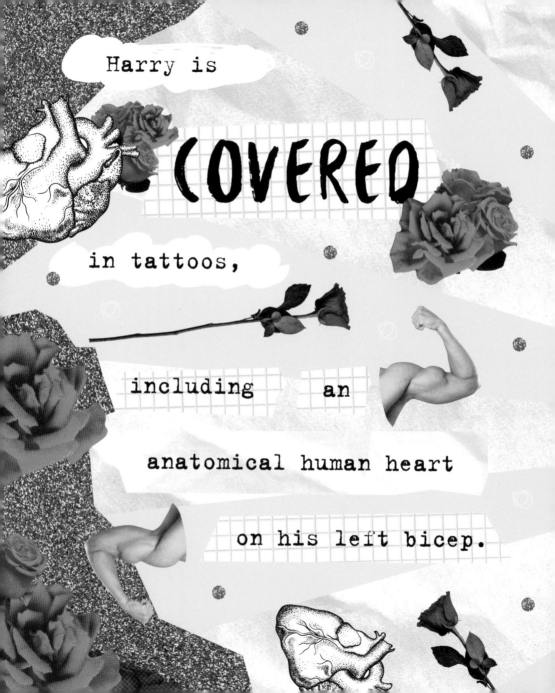

Harry is **COVERED** in tattoos, including an anatomical human heart on his left bicep.

He literally wears his heart on his sleeve.

When Harry first joined Instagram, his handle was

@GIVEMEMYNAMEPLEASE

as a cheeky

protest until the owner of

@harrystyles finally

handed over the reins.

Harry and Lizzo are OBSESSED with each other.

Nothing is more **iCONiC** than the footage of "Hizzo" flirting and giggling over **TEQUiLA** at the 2020 Brit Awards.

He made his

acting debut in

CHRISTOPHER

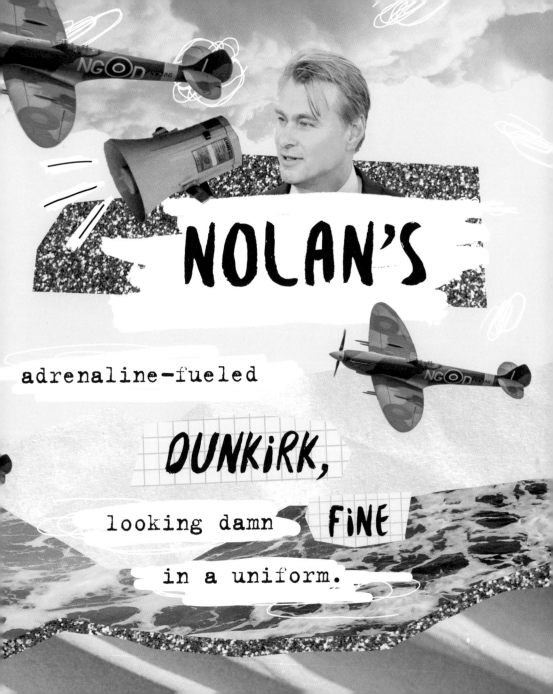

NOLAN'S

adrenaline-fueled

DUNKIRK,

looking damn FINE

in a uniform.

HARRY'S PARTIAL TO VINTAGE CARS.

He can take us for a ride around London in his primrose yellow '73 Jaguar

ANY TIME.

TELEPHONE

PULL

HE KNOWS HOW TO PARTY.

Harry bought a new mattress to celebrate

"Up All Night" topping the US charts.

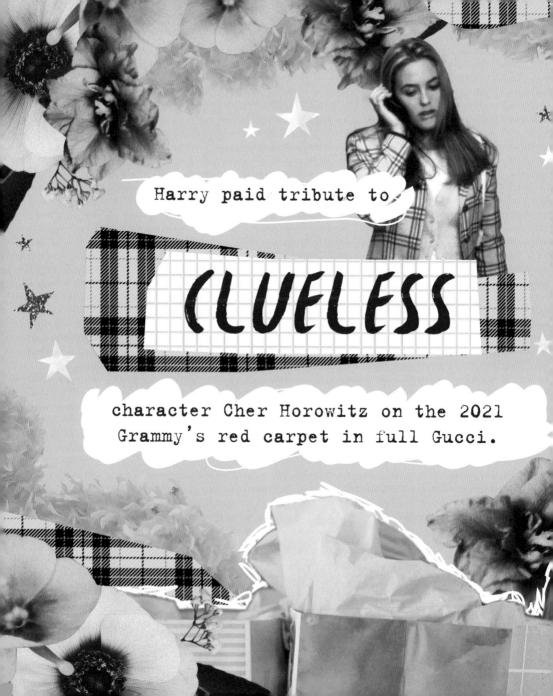

Harry paid tribute to

CLUELESS

character Cher Horowitz on the 2021 Grammy's red carpet in full Gucci.

From the plaid blazer to the purple feather boa, this look had the internet, like,

TOTALLY

BUGGIN!

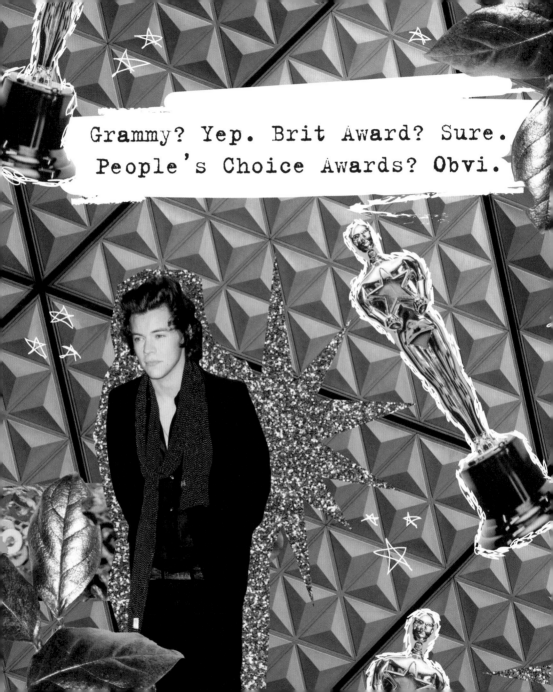

Grammy? Yep. Brit Award? Sure.
People's Choice Awards? Obvi.

Harry's surely tracking for

EGOT STATUS.

HARRY is A GENEROUS

KING!

Aside from his formal philanthropy, he used a day off in LA to buy and hand deliver $3000 worth of pizza to the homeless.

ACCORDING

TO HIS SISTER,

Harry used to wear a

hand-me-down dalmatian outfit

an INORDINATE amount

of the time'.

Despite being one of

the **BIGGEST**

pop stars on the planet,

Harry used to get

major stage fright.

And somehow that makes

him even CUTER.

His precious mum, Anne, was the one who submitted his X-Factor application.

CHEERS, MUM!

Harry really puts the

STYLE in **HARRY STYLES.**

He's risen to GOD-TIER status in the fashion world,

co-chairing the Met Gala in 2019 and becoming the first man to appear solo on a *Vogue* cover.

STEVIE NICKS

has been Harry's close friend
since they met backstage at a

FLEETWOOD MAC CONCERT in 2015.

It was Stevie's birthday, and Harry
appeared with a cake complete with
her name hand-piped on top.

Harry says that his

FRIENDSHIPS

are the most

valuable thing

in his life.

CRYING EMOJI

Once, Harry's car broke down
in front of a fan's house.
She wasn't home (can you
imagine???), but her dad let
Harry in to use the phone.

Harry left her an adorable note and even fed her fish.

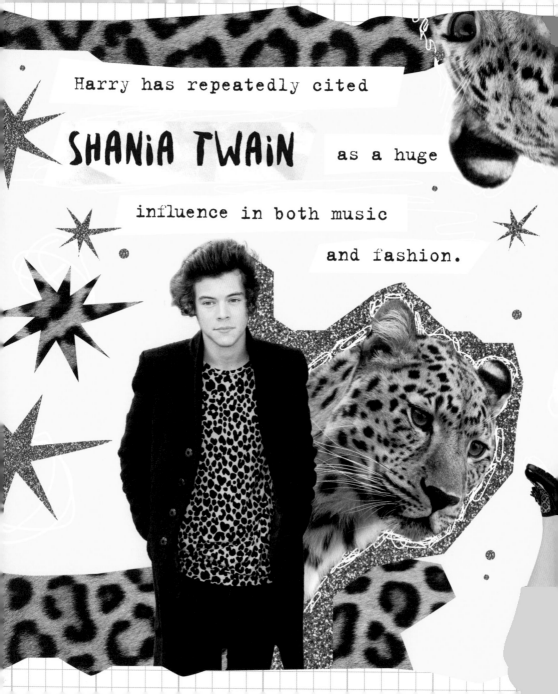

Harry has repeatedly cited

SHANiA TWAiN as a huge

influence in both music

and fashion.

You might say that she

DOES, INDEED,

impress him much.

HE'S FUNNY.

Never was this more
evident than when Harry hosted

THE LATE LATE SHOW

the day James Cordon's
daughter was born.

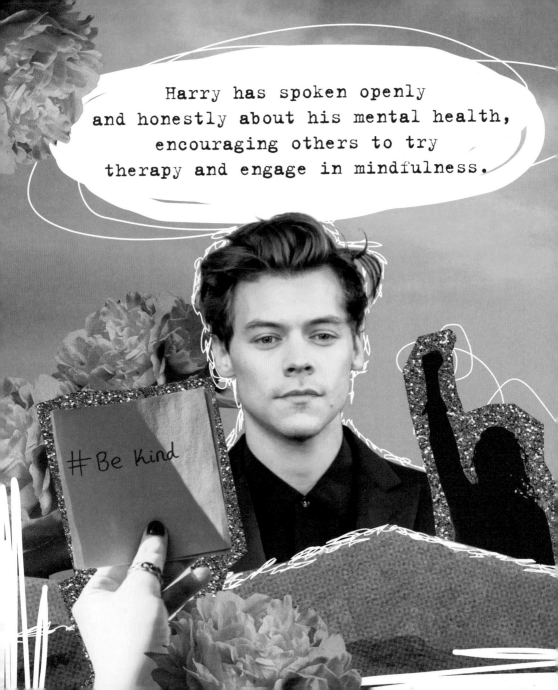

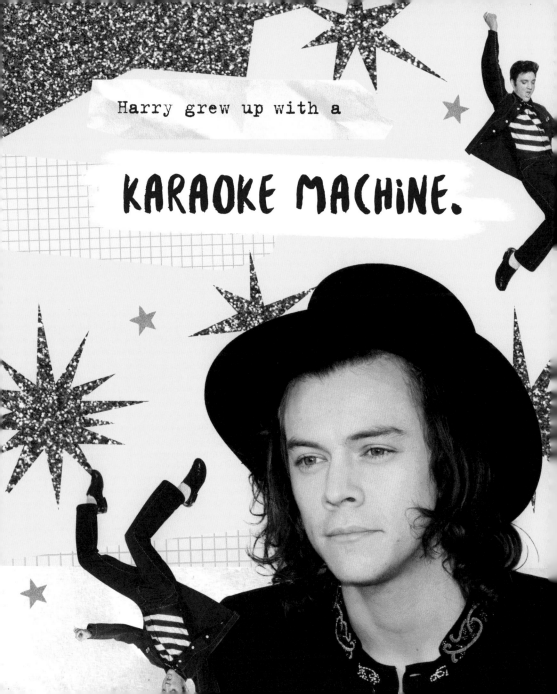

Harry grew up with a

KARAOKE MACHINE.

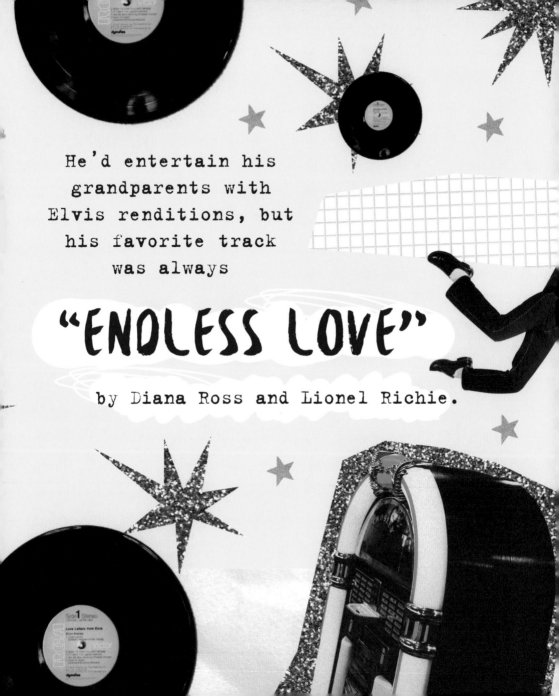

He'd entertain his grandparents with Elvis renditions, but his favorite track was always

"ENDLESS LOVE"

by Diana Ross and Lionel Richie.

"Watermelon Sugar" got the internet feelin'

HOT
AND
HEAVY,

with thirsty fans deciding

THE SONG'S LYRICS CELEBRATE

A CERTAIN

type of lovemaking.

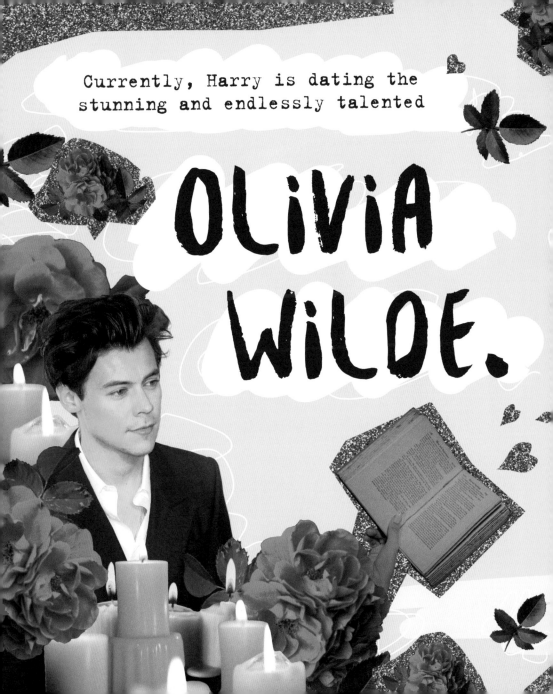

Currently, Harry is dating the stunning and endlessly talented

OLiViA WiLDE.

Together they are the power couple to end all power couples.

Harry's ever-

BLOSSOMING

solo career has defied

the trajectory

of most boy band alumni.

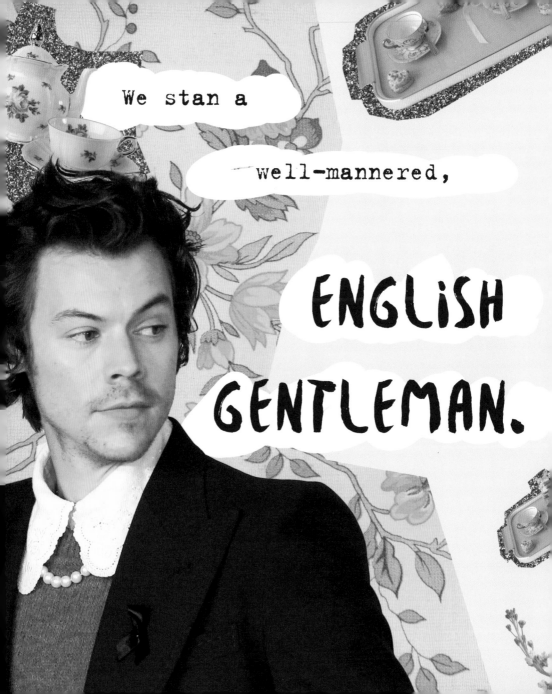

We stan a well-mannered, ENGLISH GENTLEMAN.

Harry is famously punctual and polite to everyone he meets.

FOR ANYONE

who wants
to claim

he doesn't
have talent,

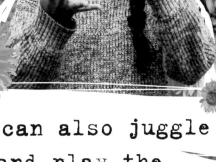

Harry can also juggle
and play the

KAZOO.

IN HiS

ONE DiRECTiON DAYS,

the band recorded their albums on the road, in a van with no air conditioning.

Harry has worked (and sweated) for his fame.

Once, Harry managed to get a rare picture beside a smiling Van Morrison.

Harry jokes that he got Van to crack a grin by tickling him on the back.

OH, TO BE THAT BACK.

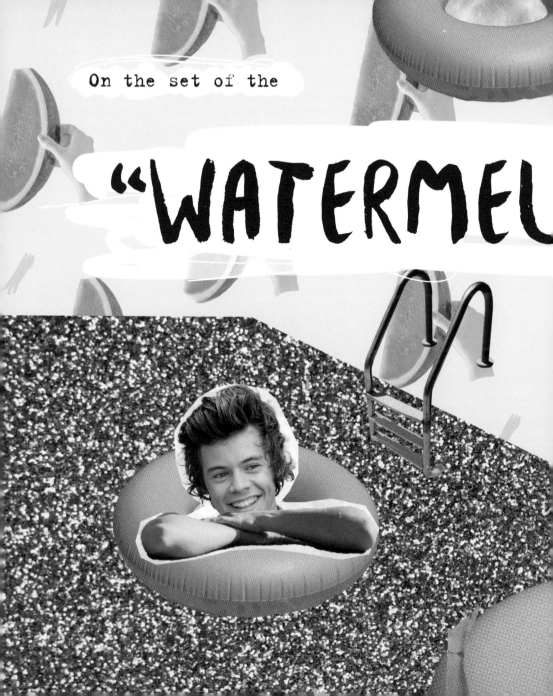

On the set of the

"WATERMEL

ON SUGAR"

music video, Harry set a clear
standard of consent for physical contact
between the cast.

WE LOVE TO SEE IT!

Harry had to **CHOP OFF HIS** luxurious One Direction **LOCKS** to film Dunkirk.

He donated his hair to a British charity that makes wigs for kids undergoing cancer treatment.

The intense online fandom surrounding Harry inspired the critically acclaimed (and stupidly funny) Australian musical Fangirls.

HE LOOOOVES APPLE JUiCE.

Harry's second solo album

FINE LINE

was included in Rolling Stone's "500 Greatest Albums

OF

ALL

TIME"

in 2020.

How many former boy band members can claim that?

His list of song writing credits includes tracks for

ARIANA GRANDE, MEGHAN TRAINOR AND MICHEAL BUBLÉ.

He's also collaborated with

TAYLOR SWIFT, JOHN LEGEND, AND BRUNO MARS.

A DAY!

Harry says a school play
might have kicked off his
flair for fashion.

He played a church mouse named
Barney and the costume included
his first-ever pair of tights.

I'm sure the performance was moving.

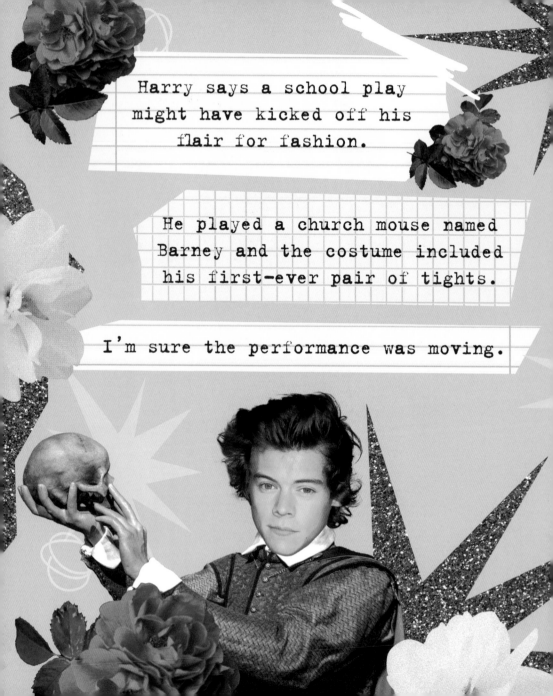

The following statement is
presented without comment:

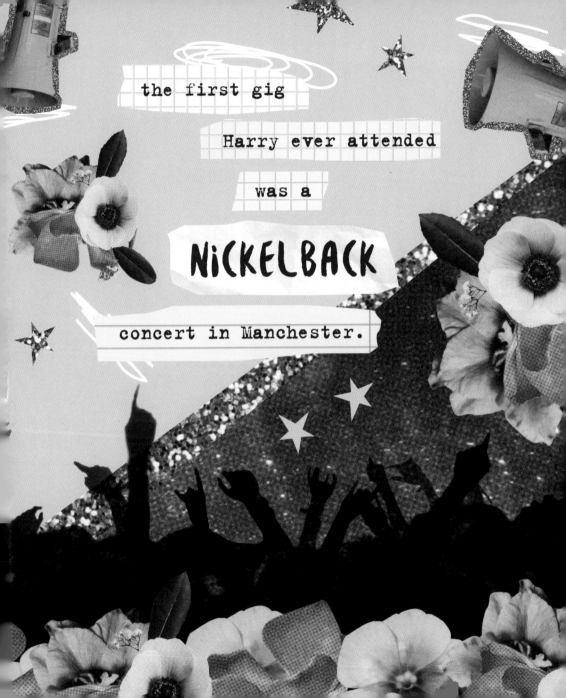

the first gig

Harry ever attended

was a

NiCKELBACK

concert in Manchester.

Harry donated

a whopping

$1.2

iLLiON

to charity after

his first solo tour.

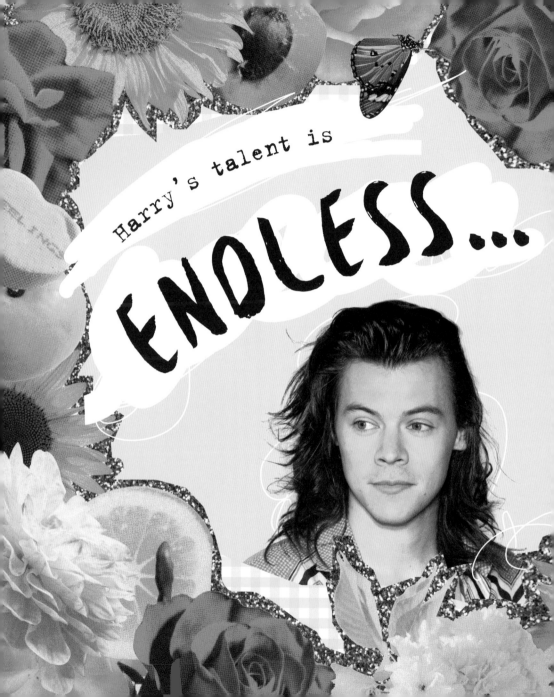

Harry's talent is

ENDLESS...

just like our love

for him.

Smith Street Books

Published in 2022 by Smith Street Books
Naarm | Melbourne | Australia
smithstreetbooks.com

ISBN: 978-1-92241-765-7

Publisher: Paul McNally
Project editor: Avery Hayes
Design and layout: George Saad & Emi Chiba
Proofreader: Hannah Koelmeyer

Printed & bound in China by C&C Offset Printing Co., Ltd.

Book 196
10 9 8 7 6 5 4 3 2 1

MIX
Paper from
responsible sources
FSC® C008047
FSC
www.fsc.org